WHISTLE-BLOWERS

EXPOSING CRIME AND CORRUPTION

MATT DOEDEN

TWENTY-FIRST CENTURY BOOKS / MINNEAPOLIS

Twenty-First Century Books
A division of Lerner Publishing Group, Inc.
241 First Avenue North
Minneapolis, MN 55401 USA

For reading levels and more information, look up this title at www.lernerbooks.com.

Main body text set in Dante MT Std 12/15.
Typeface provided by Monotype Typography.

Library of Congress Cataloging-in-Publication Data

Doeden, Matt.
    Whistle-blowers : Exposing crime and corruption / by Matt Doeden.
        pages cm
    Includes bibliographical references and index.
    ISBN 978-1-4677-4209-2 (lib. bdg. : alk. paper)
    ISBN 978-1-4677-6312-7 (EB pdf)
    1. Whistle blowing—Juvenile literature. 2. Corruption—Prevention—Juvenile literature. 3. Crime prevention—Juvenile literature. 4. Ethics—Juvenile literature.
    I. Title.
    JF1525.W45D64 2015
    364.4'1—dc23   2014011850

Manufactured in the United States of America
1 – VI – 12/31/14

TABLE OF CONTENTS

Chapter 1

Blowing the Whistle

As an employee of a top-secret US government agency, a young man is managing the massive amounts of data the agency collects. Call records. Internet browsing habits. E-mail usage. This information, he thinks, is to help federal agents uncover terrorist threats and to track down those responsible—all to protect everyday Americans and other innocent people around the globe.

He discovers that the agency is doing far more than spying on terrorists. It's spying on *everyone,* illegally collecting data on everything people do online or by phone. And the agency can use that data anytime it wants.

This isn't make-believe. It's exactly what happened to Edward Snowden in 2013 when he was working for the US National Security Agency (NSA), one of the biggest and most powerful intelligence agencies in the world. Young, exceptionally bright, and opinionated, Snowden found himself at the center of one of the biggest whistle-blowing controversies in history. He felt that because the NSA was grossly overstepping its constitutional bounds through the massive breadth of its surveillance program, he had to go public with what he knew.

Edward Snowden went public with confidential government documents in 2013 to reveal a massive and unauthorized surveillance campaign of citizens around the globe on the part of the US National Security Agency (NSA). As a firm believer in the constitutional right to privacy, Snowden felt a moral obligation to blow the whistle on the NSA.

It was a decision that led to an international manhunt, to a political standoff between two of the most powerful nations in the world, and to a massive reform of how US intelligence agencies—and intelligence agencies around the world—go about their business.

It was also a decision that put an end to life as Snowden knew it. He became a fugitive, charged with espionage and living in exile in a foreign land, perhaps forever. It made him a hero in the eyes of some and a villain and a traitor to others. All because he chose to denounce activities undertaken by the US government that he believed were illegal.

A Look Back

The term *whistle-blower* is something of a modern-day buzzword. The term didn't exist until consumer rights activist Ralph Nader coined it

Commodore Esek Hopkins played a role in the arrest of two American naval whistle-blowers in the 1770s. The situation led to the first congressional legislation to defend the right of whistle-blowers to go public with information about fraud, corruption, or other misconduct.

in the 1970s as a positive way to refer to someone who exposes confidential information. But the idea behind the word has been around for a long time. One of the first laws to protect whistle-blowers was written in the United States in 1777, during the American Revolution (1775–1783), in response to an incident in the Continental navy that winter. Commodore Esek Hopkins was the commander of the American warship *Warren*. Hopkins was born to a wealthy and politically powerful family in Rhode Island. His brother had been the state's governor and one of the signers of the Declaration of Independence.

According to his men, Commodore Hopkins treated British prisoners of war with terrible brutality, including torturing them. Ten sailors under his command gathered in a secret meeting aboard the *Warren* and wrote a petition to put an end to the torture. In it, they wrote that Hopkins "treated prisoners in the most inhuman and barbarous manner." They sent one of the men, US Marine captain John Grannis, to deliver the petition to the Continental Congress, the governing body of the United States during the revolutionary period. The congressional delegates then removed Hopkins from his post.

Hopkins fought back. In his home state of Rhode Island, he filed a criminal suit for libel against the petitioners. Two of the petitioners, Samuel Shaw and Richard Marven, were in Rhode Island at the time, and they were arrested and jailed. Infuriated by the arrest and jailing of men who had gone public with information about abhorrent behavior, the Continental Congress acted quickly. The delegates passed a law stating, "That it is the duty of all persons in the service of the United States, as well as all other inhabitants thereof, to give the earliest information to Congress or any other proper authority of any misconduct, frauds or misdemeanors committed by any officers or persons in the service of these states, which may come to their knowledge." The Congress backed up the law by authorizing to pay for the best lawyers to defend the sailors against the libel suit.

Shaw and Marven won their case and were released from jail. The Founding Fathers had sent a clear message. Those who risked their careers and their lives to expose corruption and wrongdoing deserve protection.

Obligation versus Confidence

Like Snowden and the sailors on the *Warren*, whistle-blowers have direct access to or knowledge of privileged, or confidential, information. In cases where they believe strongly that this information proves illegal, immoral, harmful, or otherwise unacceptable behaviors or practices—and they see no other way to right the wrongs—whistle-blowers go public. They reach out to journalists, government figures, business leaders, or other authorities, providing them with documents and other proof of corruption or criminal behavior. By going public with this information, whistle-blowers aim to shine a light on unacceptable actions to force change or, in some cases, to get revenge.

In making the decision about whether to blow the whistle or to remain silent, whistle-blowers weigh two main factors: social obligation versus the responsibility to protect privileged information. Privileged information is knowledge an

> In cases where they believe strongly that this information proves illegal, immoral, harmful, or otherwise unacceptable behaviors or practices— and they see no other way to right the wrongs— whistle-blowers go public.

employee or a member of an organization gains as a result of association with that company or organization. For example, accountants have access to private information about clients' income and company revenues. Doctors and other health care professionals have access to the private medical records of their patients.

With access to privileged information comes the expectation, often the requirement, of protecting the confidence, or secrecy, of that information. Accountants, doctors, and others are bound by law, under most circumstances, not to reveal confidential information about their clients and patients to outside parties. Likewise, many employees are required to sign agreements of confidentiality in which they agree not to reveal certain types of information, such as trade secrets or financial details about the company's performance. If they break their agreement by going public with protected information, they may lose their jobs or face a civil lawsuit.

But federal employees do have some laws protecting their rights to report illegal activity, and most states have additional laws to protect whistle-blowers from punishment. These laws are part of a philosophy of social obligation directing citizens to release confidential information when it could prevent or reduce harm or suffering to others. The laws vary from state to state, but in general, they protect employees from termination or punishment when reporting a company's illegal activities. For example, if an accountant blows the whistle on a company for illegal recordkeeping, whistle-blower laws can come into play to protect that person from being fired, demoted, or denied future promotions.

WHISTLEBLOWER PROTECTION ACT

In recent decades, the federal government and state governments have passed laws to protect whistle-blowers. For example, the Whistleblower Protection Act of 1989 protects federal employees from retaliation for reporting unlawful or unethical conduct.

State laws protecting whistle-blowers vary widely. The following map breaks down American whistle-blower laws.

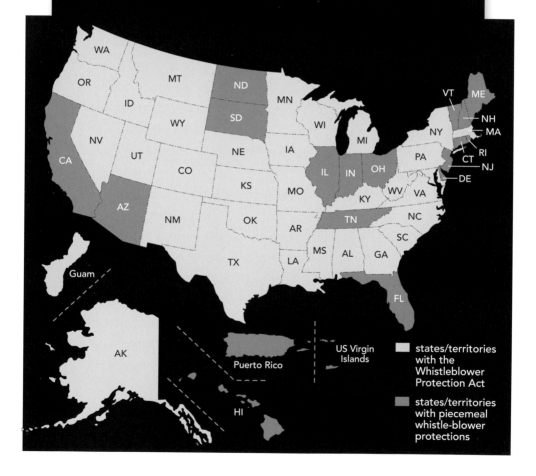

states/territories with the Whistleblower Protection Act

states/territories with piecemeal whistle-blower protections

Fallout

A would-be whistle-blower must also weigh the personal costs of the decision. The fallout can be as basic as losing the trust of an employer or of colleagues. Depending on a state's whistle-blower laws, a whistle-blower could be denied future promotions or lose a job entirely. In the Snowden case, he was charged with espionage, which carries the potential punishment of decades in prison. In extreme cases, a whistle-blower may face harassment—verbal or physical—from employers or fellow colleagues. That was the fate of New Jersey State Police officer Justin Hopson after he blew the whistle on an illegal arrest by a fellow officer. Even though he had stood up for the law and had told the truth, Hopson was continually harassed by his fellow officers, while those in charge failed to protect him. In Hopson's case, he was never fired for his actions. But work conditions became so intolerable that he was forced to leave the job he loved.

The ramifications of whistle-blowing can include loss of life. For example, in 2009, a time of political turmoil in Iran, twenty-six-year-old doctor Ramin Pourandarjani was working at the well-known and greatly feared Kahrizak Detention Center in Iran's Tehran Province. Arrest and torture of protesters at the facility was not uncommon, although the Iranian government denied all charges of torture. Yet Pourandarjani had himself treated some of the torture victims and chose to blow the whistle in the hopes of bringing the torture to an end.

An embarrassment to Iranian leaders, who are intolerant of whistle-blowing, Pourandarjani was soon arrested and jailed.

Under the threat of losing his medical license if he spoke further about the matter, he was released on bail. Ongoing threats against Pourandarjani were such that he feared for his life, and later that same year, he died under suspicious circumstances. The Iranian government officially claimed that he had died after a heart attack. Many others believed that he had been poisoned. When the Iranian government refused to allow Pourandarjani's family to pursue an autopsy to determine the real cause of death, speculation about the poisoning only intensified. Many people, both within Iran and abroad, strongly suspect that no matter the specific cause of death, Pourandarjani was killed because he had blown the whistle on the Iranian government in an extremely damaging way.

Or Are They Heroes?

By contrast, many whistle-blowers are celebrated as heroes. For example, in 2001 Sherron Watkins was working as a vice president of corporate development at the offices of Enron Corporation, an energy company based in Houston, Texas. The company was active in buying and selling energy-based commodities such as natural gas. Watkins discovered gross financial fraud at the company. Enron was falsifying its revenue and lying to investors about the success of some of its companies in an effort to keep stock prices rising. After going to her supervisors with what she knew—and being rebuffed—she chose to blow the whistle, first, by informing top Enron officials about the practices and, later, by testifying before the US Congress.

"What makes truth uncomfortable? It is uncomfortable when we ignore it, when we suppress it, when we hide from it. Why did so many at Enron keep silent about shoddy accounting practices? Basically, because they got a swift and painful smack to the forehead when they did speak up."

—*Sherron Watkins, 2008*

Although some people criticized her for waiting as long as she did to alert government authorities about what she knew, Watkins was widely praised for her actions. In 2002 *Time* named her one of the magazine's three Persons of the Year, along with two other whistle-blowers, Cynthia Cooper of WorldCom and Coleen Rowley of the Federal Bureau of Investigation (FBI). Enron filed bankruptcy in 2001 and eventually went out of business. Watkins has gone on to shape a career as a respected expert on ethics and leadership.

In 2001 Sherron Watkins, a vice president at Enron Corporation, blew the whistle on accounting irregularities within the company. She left Enron the next year and went on to co-author *Power Failure: The Inside Story of the Collapse of Enron*, published in 2003.

PERSONS OF THE YEAR

Sherron Watkins was named one of *Time's* three Persons of the Year in 2002 for blowing the whistle on Enron. Two other women, Cynthia Cooper and Coleen Rowley *(above)*, shared the honor with her.

Cooper's story is quite similar to Watkins's. Cooper was the vice president of internal audit at WorldCom, a telecommunications company. Like Watkins, Cooper uncovered massive fraud in how WorldCom was reporting revenue. Cooper and several colleagues were determined to uncover the fraud. They often worked late at night, pouring over the company's books, to avoid detection by their bosses. In the end, they blew the whistle on about $3.8 billion of phony accounting entries, making it the largest case at that time of corporate fraud.

Rowley, meanwhile, was a special agent with the FBI. She was investigating the case of suspected terrorist Zacarias Moussaoui, who is believed to have been in training to fly one of the planes in the terrorist attacks of September 11, 2001. Through her work, Rowley discovered that the FBI had received key evidence about the plot well before the attacks took place. However, the agency had badly mishandled the information and had not taken action on what it knew. Rowley testified before the US Senate and the 9/11 Commission, and her actions led to a major reform in the internal organization of the FBI. A new FBI Office of Intelligence was launched, hiring additional staff with counterterrorism and language skills.

PERSONS OF THE YEAR

The Whistleblowers

CYNTHIA COOPER
OF WORLDCOM

COLEEN ROWLEY
OF THE FBI

SHERRON WATKINS
OF ENRON

Time chooses a person of the year to feature on the cover of the magazine's special year-end edition. Historically, the magazine has recognized very few women. In 2002 *Time* chose three whistle-blowers, all of whom were women, for that year's Persons of the Year edition. From left to right are Cynthia Cooper, Coleen Rowley, and Sherron Watkins.

Chapter 2

Deep Throat: Bringing Down a President

Politics and scandal sometimes go hand in hand. One of the greatest and most famous examples is the case known simply as Watergate. And it's possible that nothing would have come to light if not for a whistle-blower who was for three decades known only as Deep Throat.

The Scandal

At the core of the Watergate scandal was a 1972 burglary at the Watergate Hotel complex in Washington, DC. That spring the Republican Party was hard at work on the reelection campaign of President Richard Nixon. Some of Nixon's top aides were committed to ensuring victory, at whatever cost. They wanted to leave nothing to chance. A plan emerged to break into the headquarters of the Democratic National Committee (DNC), located in the Watergate complex. There, burglars would copy data and bug the office. This would allow them to closely monitor DNC campaign tactics and to develop effective responses.

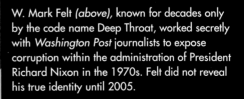

W. Mark Felt *(above)*, known for decades only by the code name Deep Throat, worked secretly with *Washington Post* journalists to expose corruption within the administration of President Richard Nixon in the 1970s. Felt did not reveal his true identity until 2005.

On May 28, burglars broke into the DNC headquarters late at night. They photographed documents and attached wiretaps to the phones of key DNC leaders. Their mission was a success. But they wanted more. So the burglars returned on June 17. This time, everything went wrong. A hotel security guard noticed that the door latches to the DNC office had been taped over to prevent the doors from locking. The guard called the police, who captured and arrested five men: locksmith Virgilio González, undercover agents Bernard Barker and Frank Sturgis, Central Intelligence Agency (CIA) agent James McCord Jr., and political activist Eugenio Martínez. All were loyal to the Republican Party.

Suspicion quickly fell on Nixon's aides and the Republican Party, all of whom staunchly denied involvement in the burglary. Ronald L. Ziegler, the White House press secretary, dismissed the event as a "third-rate burglary." Nixon immediately began to cover his tracks. He used intimidation and threats to keep people—even his closest aides—silent.

Media coverage of the scandal was intense, and much of the key reporting came from *Time* magazine, the *New York Times*, and Bob Woodward and Carl Bernstein, a team of young investigative journalists for the *Washington Post*. Woodward and Bernstein were very familiar with Nixon from covering his reelection campaign, and they immediately suspected that the scandal ran deep—the FBI, the CIA, and even the White House were all involved.

The two reporters dropped their first bombshell on June 19, 1972, just two days after the second break-in. They reported that one of the men who had been arrested, McCord, was in charge of security for Nixon's reelection and fund-raising organization, known as the Committee to Re-Elect the President (CREEP). McCord's connection to Nixon was not definitive proof that the White House had been involved, but it was a key piece connecting the crime to the Oval Office.

Enter Mark Felt

Meanwhile, the FBI had been conducting its own investigation into the break-in. The highest officials at the FBI, including associate director Mark Felt, Sr., had already uncovered the connection between McCord and the president, as well as other evidence that pointed to the Nixon administration's active role in the plot. Felt was impressed with Woodward and Bernstein's work, and he resolved to help them bring the rest of the cover-up story to light.

Bob Woodward *(left)* and Carl Bernstein *(right)* broke the Watergate story in the *Washington Post* in June 1972. As a result of their investigative reporting, the *Post* won the Pulitzer Prize for Public Service in 1973. The two men went on to write a book about the Watergate story called *All the President's Men*, which was made into a film in 1976. The popular, now classic, movie stars Robert Redford as Woodward and Dustin Hoffman as Bernstein.

Felt secretly contacted the reporters to arrange a series of meetings in a deserted parking garage. The first occurred on June 20—just three days after the burglary and the arrests. Felt didn't tell the reporters outright everything they wanted to know. But he did point them in the right direction, urging them to follow certain leads, especially the trail of money that would ultimately prove the Nixon administration's involvement.

Felt understood that going public with information from an ongoing FBI investigation would mark a swift end to his career. And it could even result in criminal charges against him. So he insisted on, and the reporters agreed to, Felt's complete anonymity in return for help in the journalists' investigation. Toward that end, a *Post* editor gave Felt the nickname Deep Throat. Woodward later described Felt's frame of mind about blowing the whistle. "[He] had clearly been torn, and even uncertain—not fully convinced that helping us was the proper course, wanting both to do it and not do it. . . . He wanted to be protected at nearly any cost, and he had gone to extraordinary lengths to conceal his identity."

SECRET SIGNALS

Mark Felt didn't dare to communicate openly with *Washington Post* journalists Woodward and Bernstein. So the trio set up a system of secret signals. When Woodward wanted a meeting, he would place a flowerpot with a red flag on the balcony of his apartment. When Felt wanted a meeting, he would make a mark on page 20 of Woodward's copy of the *New York Times*. They usually met in the very early hours of the morning in an underground parking garage in nearby Rosslyn, Virginia.

"He knew he was taking a monumental risk."

—journalist Bob Woodward, 2005, on Mark Felt's decision to help the Washington Post *investigation into the Watergate scandal*

With Felt's help, the reporters' investigation took off. They followed the money trail, searching for links between the arrested burglars and the Nixon administration. Among the connections they uncovered was a check for $25,000, written as a donation to Nixon's reelection campaign but deposited instead into the account of one of the burglars (Bernard Barker). Over the coming months, Woodward and Bernstein's reporting—much of it as a result of Felt's insider information—painted an increasingly damaging portrait of the Nixon administration's willingness to subvert the law to ensure a second term for the president and to cover up any and all illegal efforts to make that happen. Woodward later commented about the working relationship with Felt. "I was thankful for any morsel of information, confirmation, or assistance Felt gave me while [Bernstein] and I were attempting to understand the many-headed monster of Watergate. . . . Because of his position virtually atop the chief investigative agency, his words and guidance had immense, at times even staggering, authority."

Yet despite the growing evidence that Nixon's administration had illegally broken into and spied on the DNC, the American public initially remained ignorant of the scandal. So in November 1972, Nixon didn't simply win reelection—he won by one of the largest margins in the twentieth century.

The Fallout

Nixon won the election, but the noose continued to tighten around him and his aides. The US Senate was forming the Senate Watergate Committee to investigate the incident, and on January 30, 1973, just ten days after Nixon's inauguration ceremony, two of Nixon's former aides—attorney G. Gordon Liddy and CIA agent McCord—were convicted of conspiracy, burglary, and wiretapping in the Watergate burglaries. In April 1973, McCord began cooperating with the congressional investigation and confirmed that the burglars' orders had indeed come from the White House. Soon thereafter, several of Nixon's top aides resigned their positions, knowing that the spotlight would soon focus on them. Nixon remained defiant. In November 1973, with the heat of the investigation at a peak, he famously declared to the American public, which by this time was following the scandal closely, "I am not a crook!"

The evidence against Nixon was overwhelming. Yet he continued to thwart investigators by refusing to turn over evidence to the Watergate Committee. Evidence included key audiotape recordings of Oval Office conversations that investigators believed would tie the president directly to the cover-up. With public and political support for Nixon plummeting, Congress began deliberating whether to impeach the president. The live impeachment hearings were televised in late July 1974, and Americans were riveted. It quickly became clear that the committee—and eventually the House of Representatives—would vote to impeach, and even Nixon could see the writing on the wall. On August 8, 1974, Nixon addressed the nation on live television to announce that he would resign

Richard Nixon was the first and only American president to resign from office. Facing impeachment as a result of the Watergate scandal, he announced his resignation on live television on August 8, 1974.

from office, effective at noon the next day. Nixon entered US history as the first president to resign from office. Vice President Gerald Ford automatically assumed the presidency to finish out Nixon's term, and a month later, on September 8, Ford pardoned Nixon of all crimes for which he had been accused.

Impact

The Watergate scandal served as a warning to legislators that the system of checks and balances on presidential power, established by the nation's founders, wasn't enough to curb abuse of presidential authority. Congress responded by passing a series of additional laws. Among them were changes to the

Freedom of Information Act, designed to allow easier access to presidential documents to make White House activities more transparent. Politically, the backlash against the Republican Party was severe at both national and state levels. The Democrats dominated the elections of 1976, with Georgia's Democratic governor Jimmy Carter winning the presidential election that year. Perhaps the most lasting impact was the loss of trust in the American president. It's a trust that has never been fully restored.

Felt's Fate

Deep Throat's true identity remained a secret even after the Watergate scandal faded away into history. Woodward and Bernstein had promised anonymity, and they held to that promise. Over the decades, many names—Felt's among them— surfaced as possible candidates, but no one ever managed to pin down the real source of Woodward and Bernstein's information. Felt himself published his memoirs in 1979, adamantly denying that he was Deep Throat.

The great mystery finally ended in May 2005 when Felt stepped forward. "I'm the guy they used to call Deep Throat," Felt said in *Vanity Fair* magazine. In poor health and not knowing how much longer he had to live, Felt finally admitted to being the world's most famous whistle-blower. While some critics blasted Felt for his actions and for his motives for bringing down a president, the overwhelming reaction was positive. Felt died in 2008 at the age of ninety-five.

Why Did He Do It?

High-level intelligence agents such as Felt don't come lightly to the decision to blow the whistle. Keeping secrets is a part of their job. So why did Felt decide to blow the whistle in this case? Years later, Woodward described Felt's motives as pure. According to Woodward, Felt believed that Nixon's "lawless presidency" was endangering the nation.

For many, this explanation is sufficient. It plays out as an appealing story of an American hero defending justice and bringing down a corrupt president. Yet a closer look reveals that while Felt may indeed have disapproved of the Nixon White House, personal motivations may have been just as powerful. By leaking information to the reporters, Felt may have been playing a very high-stakes game to further his own career.

When longtime FBI director J. Edgar Hoover died in May 1972, Felt believed that he deserved to take over Hoover's role as director. Instead, the Nixon administration selected a rival, L. Patrick Gray. Felt was furious. By carefully leaking information to Woodward and Bernstein, Felt was able to damage the reputations of both the administration that had overlooked him for a job he coveted as well as the man they had chosen for the job. Some have even speculated that the White House knew Felt was the leak but did not act for fear he would divulge even more damaging information.

We may never entirely understand Felt's motivations. In this case, one man's anger over a missed job opportunity—and his passion for protecting democracy—came together as the combustible fuel that brought down a president.

Chapter 3

Exposing Big Tobacco: Jeffrey Wigand Takes On Brown & Williamson

Jeffrey Wigand was not a typical tobacco executive when the Brown & Williamson (B&W) tobacco company hired him in 1988 as vice president of research and development. Wigand had built his résumé in health care—about as far from tobacco as one can get. Yet B&W hoped to capitalize on Wigand's biochemistry background and on his knowledge of medical devices and pharmaceuticals. At a time when the national spotlight on the dangers of smoking cigarettes was intensifying, B&W put him in charge of developing a cigarette with fewer harmful side effects.

At first, Wigand was excited about the idea of making a safer cigarette. He guided B&W research teams, investigating the harmful chemicals found in cigarettes and looking for safer alternatives. But over time, B&W executives grew less interested in the project and Wigand began to grow suspicious of the company's real intentions. It seemed the company wanted to sweep the safe cigarette idea under the rug and continue with the status quo, which meant promoting a product the company knew was addictive and harmful to consumers' health.

As a tobacco industry insider, Jeffrey Wigand blew the whistle on Big Tobacco. He exposed the ways in which the tobacco company for which he worked—Brown & Williamson—was covering up the known health risks of tobacco use. He has won a variety of awards and honors for distinguished service and management ethics since that time and gives lectures on tobacco-related health issues all over the world.

Conflict

As the head of research and development, Wigand had access to a wealth of information. Although the company denied it publicly, Wigand knew that B&W had documented the addictive properties of tobacco as well as the known health risks, including cancer, of some of the chemicals that were in B&W products. Yet the company kept quiet about these dangers to protect sales.

Wigand often found himself in conflict with B&W executives. He quickly learned that many others in the company did not share his enthusiasm for safety. For example, when he provided the company's chief executive officer (CEO) with evidence that coumarin, an additive in a popular line of B&W pipe tobacco, caused tumors in mice, his warnings were ignored. According to Wigand, he was told to remain quiet about the dangers. Removing the additive would affect the taste of the tobacco and could, therefore, negatively affect sales. Wigand continued to protest, and in March 1993, he was fired.

B&W gave Wigand a severance package, which included health benefits for his family. In exchange, Wigand signed a confidentiality agreement forbidding him to talk about the things he'd learned while working for B&W. Yet Wigand didn't remain as silent as B&W executives would have liked. For example, he discussed his severance package with a colleague—a violation of the agreement, according to the company. He also agreed to serve as a consultant for the CBS news program *60 Minutes* on a story about cigarettes and fire safety. Meanwhile, the US Congress was holding hearings regarding the safety of cigarettes and tobacco. When B&W chief executive officers stood before Congress, swearing they did not believe cigarettes were addictive, Wigand was appalled.

He was ready to go further with what he knew, providing damaging information about the tobacco industry to officials with the Food and Drug Administration. According to Wigand, when B&W found out, the company began an attempt to threaten and intimidate him into silence. He claims the company stopped at nothing to make his life miserable, charging that B&W agents followed him, stalked him at his Kentucky home, and terrorized him with harassing and threatening messages and phone calls. Wigand claims that B&W agents went so far as to place a bullet inside his mailbox as a threat against his life. (B&W officials denied this.) According to Wigand, company agents even threatened his children. Fearing for his life and the safety of his family, Wigand began carrying a handgun.

In addition, because he had by this time been blacklisted as a whistle-blower, Wigand couldn't get work in his field. So he took a teaching job at a local high school. It paid $30,000 a year—a fraction of the roughly $300,000 annual salary he had earned at B&W and on which he had built a life for himself and his family. As Wigand's fortunes plummeted, he was forced to sell the family home and was soon separated from his wife.

Time to Talk

Wigand was a man with a temper, and he deeply resented the treatment he was receiving from his former employer. So he made up his mind—agreement or not, he was going to tell the world what he knew.

Wigand's motives were multilayered. Partly, he wanted to right the injustice he knew was endemic to the world of

Big Tobacco. But as much as he cared about protecting public health, he also wanted to protect his own image and to defend his battered pride. B&W had pushed him too far and too hard, and Wigand wasn't willing to take it quietly. He later explained, "[My decision to come forward with what I knew] was based on a lot of things. I didn't like how my agreement with Brown & Williamson was turning into a form of extortion. I didn't like being threatened. . . . And it just really made me mad to see the tobacco CEOs lying in front of Congress."

"What is the obligation one has with knowledge? When you have knowledge you have a responsibility to use that knowledge. With particularly negative knowledge, hard knowledge that I had . . . of documents having been destroyed, companies targeting children, creating an addiction that leads to illness and doing all that for profit. That's wrong. So, [speaking out] was a morally right decision."

—Jeffrey Wigand, 2013

So Wigand spoke again to the producers of *60 Minutes*. He went to New York to sit down with broadcasting legend Mike Wallace in a tell-all interview. The news program planned to air Wigand's interview with a larger future segment about the tobacco industry. In the interview, Wigand explained how tobacco executives were ignoring health concerns and lying about the dangers they knew were associated with smoking. He described a meeting at B&W in which researchers discussed the safer cigarette project. Yet when the official meeting minutes came back, B&W lawyers had edited out almost everything related to the project. "When you say you're going to have a safer cigarette, that [is a way of admitting that] everything else that you have available . . . is unsafe," Wigand explained.

His portrayal of B&W directly contradicted what tobacco executives had told Congress under oath. In short, Wigand was saying that B&W executives had lied under oath, thereby committing the punishable offense of perjury.

Wigand knew he would pay a hefty price for talking. B&W's lawyers had persuaded a Kentucky court to issue a gag order (official court order not to talk), which Wigand had ignored. That meant he could be arrested and jailed when he returned home. And his television interview ensured that he would remain forever blacklisted. No one would ever hire him in a research and development role again.

Yet the drama was not over. B&W hired investigators to dig up everything Wigand had ever done wrong, professionally and personally, in an effort to further discredit him. They referred to him as the Master of Deceit, and suddenly, every mistake Wigand had ever made became public knowledge.

Meanwhile, lawyers for B&W were doing everything they could to prevent the *60 Minutes* interview from airing. They threatened to sue CBS for interfering with Wigand's legal agreement with B&W. The network relented, fearing an expensive lawsuit, and forced Wallace to air his Big Tobacco segment with an edited version of the Wigand interview that left out the most damning details.

It was a dark, ugly time for Wigand. He had lost his career, his family, and his good name. In addition, B&W was suing him for theft, breach of contract, and fraud. Questioning his decision to step forward, Wigand turned to alcohol.

The Truth Comes Out

In early 1996, the *Wall Street Journal* published a story that included most of the information that *60 Minutes* had declined to broadcast. Most of it came from testimony Wigand had given in a Mississippi court, when he served as a witness for the state in a lawsuit against Big Tobacco. The newspaper also documented B&W's attempt to smear Wigand's name, while giving space to B&W's claim that Wigand had manufactured or exaggerated some of his claims against the company. With the information fully public, CBS executives no longer felt threatened by potential litigation from B&W, and *60 Minutes* finally aired the full Wigand interview on February 4, 1996.

THE INSIDER

In 1999 Touchstone Pictures released *The Insider*. The film tells the story of Wigand (played by Russell Crowe) and *60 Minutes* producer Lowell Bergman (Al Pacino) bringing Wigand's charges against Big Tobacco to the public. The film was well received by critics and was nominated for seven Academy Awards, including Best Picture and Best Actor (Crowe).

Making a Difference

Wigand's testimony, along with government pressure and unrelenting media coverage, forever changed smoking culture in the United States and eventually in other parts of the world. In 1998 the lawsuits brought by the attorneys general of forty-six states against the four major US tobacco companies ended with the Tobacco Master Settlement Agreement, a massive settlement—in favor of the states—worth $368 billion. As part of the deal, B&W dropped its lawsuit against Wigand.

The landmark settlement marked the beginning of a decline for big tobacco companies. Much of the settlement money was earmarked for furthering antismoking campaigns. Within a few years, the prevalence of smoking was on a sharp decline, especially among young people. In 1997, before the settlement, 36.4 percent of high school students surveyed admitted to regular tobacco use. Fourteen years later, that number had been cut in half, to 18.1 percent.

In the end, Wigand thrived as a teacher and was named Kentucky Teacher of the Year in 1996. He has since retired and remains a major force in the movement to prevent smoking among teenagers. He travels the world as an expert witness in tobacco lawsuits and formed an organization, Smoke-Free Kids, that focuses on antismoking education. "I don't think I've been this happy in a long time," Wigand said in a 2005 interview. "I enjoy what I do, and I'm comfortable with myself. Every day, I know I've [done] something that makes a difference for another human being. And that makes you feel good."

Chapter 4

Corrupt Peacekeepers: Exposing Human Trafficking in Bosnia

In 1998 Kathryn Bolkovac was a nine-year veteran of the Lincoln, Nebraska, police force when she ran into a situation that most officers dread. A suspect she was chasing pulled a knife on her, forcing her to draw her gun in self-protection. Bolkovac pulled the trigger, wounding the suspect.

The suspect lived. But the event impacted Bolkovac deeply. The shooting, combined with struggles in her personal life, led her to a decision. It was time for a change. That was when she came across a job listing for DynCorp Aerospace, part of DynCorp International, a private military contractor based in the United Kingdom that does most of its business with the US government. The job Bolkovac applied for and got was as a monitor with the International Police Task Force, a United Nations (UN) peacekeeping force in the war-ravaged nation of Bosnia.

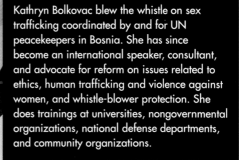

Kathryn Bolkovac blew the whistle on sex trafficking coordinated by and for UN peacekeepers in Bosnia. She has since become an international speaker, consultant, and advocate for reform on issues related to ethics, human trafficking and violence against women, and whistle-blower protection. She does trainings at universities, nongovernmental organizations, national defense departments, and community organizations.

The pay was good, and the chance to see a new part of the world—one in which her family had its roots—was irresistible. She resigned from the Lincoln Police Department and signed up with DynCorp.

Dark Discoveries

DynCorp's job in Bosnia was to help hire and train local police officers in Bosnia. The nation was recovering from the deep wounds of a bitter and bloody ethnic war that had raged there from 1992 until 1995. UN ground troops, along with bombing campaigns coordinated by North Atlantic Treaty Organization forces, had brought the war to an end. Peacekeeping arms of both international alliances then turned to helping the nation reestablish peaceful civilian life. Bolkovac was eager to get started in the effort and to make a difference for the better.

Yet Bolkovac soon learned that not all the peacekeeping forces shared her interest in protecting civilians. She got her first clue that something was wrong in Bosnia even before she left the United States. During her predeparture training in Fort Worth, Texas, she overheard another DynCorp employee bragging about how great Bosnia was, including that he knew where to go to have sex with girls as young as twelve. At first, Bolkovac didn't believe what she'd heard. She convinced herself that she had misunderstood or that the man had been making a bad joke.

In June 1999, she traveled to Sarajevo, Bosnia, to begin her work. Her experience as a police officer, along with a strong work ethic, quickly earned her a leading role in the human rights department of the International Police Task Force, where she specialized in domestic abuse cases. Her job, in part, was to work with women and children who had been raped during the war, as well as with postwar victims. It was a daunting task in a nation scarred by mass killings and genocide.

Bolkovac saw almost right away that prostitution was widespread in the region. Over time, she uncovered crimes far darker. Like other nations with desperate populations ravaged by war, Bosnia had become a center for human trafficking— the buying and selling of human beings. In particular, women and girls, mostly from economically depressed Russia and Ukraine, were being forced to work as sex slaves in Bosnian bars and brothels set up especially for peacekeepers and police officers. Local police and citizens, as well as other international employees, also participated as "clients" of the enslaved women. Those who refused to prostitute themselves were often beaten, raped, or even killed.

Resistance at Every Turn

When Bolkovac brought this information up the chain of command, she was shocked by the reaction. Many already knew what was going on, and few seemed interested in putting an end to the practice. As Bolkovac dug deeper, the discoveries grew even darker. Few resources were devoted to investigate the crimes, and in some cases, the people who were charged with investigating were taking bribes from traffickers to look the other way. One investigating officer had even paid to keep a young girl in his apartment for his own prostitution racket. "I was shocked, appalled and disgusted," Bolkovac later explained. "They were supposed to be over there to help, but they were committing crimes themselves. But when I told the supervisors they didn't want to know."

Bolkovac tried again and again to bring this information to light, but she met resistance at every turn. DynCorp itself stood to lose its lucrative contract with the US State Department if Bolkovac's discoveries were made public. And Bosnian officials weren't eager to help either. If the details of sex trafficking were exposed publicly, the nation stood to lose important US aid monies. Within days of presenting her findings, Bolkovac was ordered to cease her investigation. Death threats soon followed.

"I never thought that my international law enforcement career would be destroyed for telling the truth and seeking justice."

—Kathryn Bolkovac, 2013

But Bolkovac refused to give up. She was determined to put an end to the practice, no matter what it took. "Every other method I had tried within the scope of my job had fallen on deaf ears," Bolkovac later wrote in her book *The Whistleblower: Sex Trafficking, Military Contractors, and One Woman's Fight for Justice* (2011). "I still subscribed to the view that if I could educate my coworkers about the seriousness of their actions, then the behavior might change."

So she gathered her evidence and sent a mass e-mail to DynCorp employees and executives detailing all she knew about the role of so-called peacekeepers in Bosnian sex trafficking. The subject line of her e-mail read, "Do not read this if you have a weak stomach or a guilty conscience." Soon after the e-mail went out, DynCorp fired Bolkovac, claiming she had lied on her timesheets about how many hours she was working.

The Fallout

Bolkovac's career in international law enforcement was over. But that didn't mean she was done fighting. She sued DynCorp for unfair dismissal, traveling to the United Kingdom to testify before a British employment tribunal. The tribunal judges agreed that DynCorp had fired Bolkovac unfairly, awarding her $175,000 in damages. For DynCorp, the damages handed down by the court barely registered as a slap on the wrist. It had little effect on DynCorp's day-to-day operations or on its bottom line. DynCorp continues to work with the US military and State Department, with annual revenues of around $3 billion.

NOT ALONE

Bolkovac isn't the only DynCorp worker to blow the whistle on the sex trafficking in Bosnia. Ben Johnston was an airplane mechanic working for DynCorp in Bosnia. In 1999 he blew the whistle on coworkers' involvement in human trafficking, forced prostitution, and rape. Like Bolkovac, Johnston was fired for his actions and went on to sue the company. DynCorp admitted no wrongdoing in the case. Johnston and the company later settled out of court.

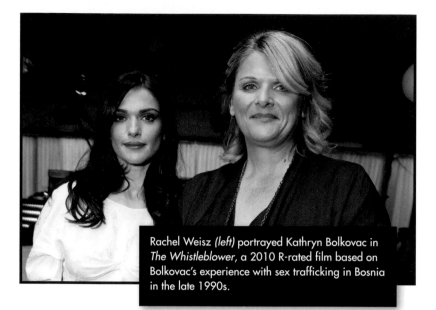

Rachel Weisz *(left)* portrayed Kathryn Bolkovac in *The Whistleblower,* a 2010 R-rated film based on Bolkovac's experience with sex trafficking in Bosnia in the late 1990s.

Likewise, the consequences to the peacekeeping forces who had participated in the trafficking were minimal. DynCorp sent several of the accused home. But because UN forces have diplomatic immunity, they cannot be charged for their crimes. The human trafficking scandal in Bosnia—and similar troubles in the Democratic Republic of Congo, Haiti, and other nations with peacekeeping forces—pushed the UN to rethink how it deals with peacekeepers who commit crimes of a sexual nature. In 2003 the UN enacted a zero-tolerance policy toward perpetrators, and in 2007, the organization introduced conduct units geared specifically toward ending such behavior. Six years later, as part of a global initiative to battle global sex trafficking, US president Barack Obama introduced a policy that would strengthen whistle-blower rights for people in situations similar to the one in which Bolkovac found herself. Yet despite these initial efforts, the problem remains rampant. New, revamped policies often prove difficult to enforce or are insufficiently forceful, and abuse continues.

Continuing Her Work

Bolkovac has since used her experience to raise awareness of human trafficking around the globe. She works to educate students and peacekeeping forces about the problem. She also pushes for reform on whistle-blower protection laws and for greater government transparency. Meanwhile, Bolkovac's story has reached millions through the 2010 film *The Whistleblower*, starring Rachel Weisz as Bolkovac, and through Bolkovac's book of the same name.

Chapter 5

A Rookie's Decision: Exposing Corruption in Law Enforcement

In March 2002, Justin Hopson was living his dream of a career in law enforcement. Years of schooling and training had finally paid off, and Hopson had been hired as a trooper with the New Jersey State Police. At that time, the police force was facing accusations of sexism and racism. Hopson knew that the officers were a very tight-knit and guarded group. But he also believed he could make a difference for the better and was eager to get started.

Just eleven days into his new career, on March 12, 2002, Hopson was riding in a patrol car with his training officer. As they hit the streets, Hopson couldn't have known that his career and his life were about to change forever.

Justin Hopson *(far left)* is sworn in as an officer with the New Jersey State Police in 2002. With less than two weeks on the job, Hopson witnessed his training officer make an unlawful arrest. Because he refused to corroborate the officer's official account of the arrest, he faced brutal harassment from a group of fellow officers known as the Lords of Discipline. Hopson blew the whistle on the group's violent behavior.

Unlawful Arrest

As a rookie with his training officer, Patrick Cole, Hopson understood his role—keep his mouth shut and observe. Late at night, the two officers spotted a man driving a red car with an expired registration. He had two female passengers with him in the vehicle. Yet when the two troopers caught up to the car in an unlit trailer park, the man was gone. Only two young women—clearly intoxicated—remained in the car. Hopson's commanding officer slapped handcuffs on one of the women and placed her under arrest for driving under the influence (DUI) of alcohol—an unlawful arrest, because the woman had not been driving the car. He then brought the other passenger into the backseat of the squad car and instructed Hopson to check the car for drugs.

"I saw this unlawful DUI arrest, and I had to make a decision to either go along with it or go alone," Hopson later recalled. But Hopson didn't make that decision right away. In his 2012 book, *Breaking the Blue Wall: One Man's War against Police Corruption*, Hopson says he briefly entertained the idea of slapping handcuffs on his training officer. But he didn't do that. Instead, he went to wait for a tow truck to haul the red car away from the scene.

Later that night, when his shift was over, Hopson struggled with what he'd seen. He understood that calling out his training officer would put him in the bad graces of some of his fellow officers. But after speaking with his father on the phone, Hopson knew what he had to do. What he'd witnessed was an unlawful arrest, and as a sworn officer of the law, he had to speak up.

A Thousand Cuts

Officers of the law create and sign written reports of each arrest they make. The day after the arrest, Hopson told Cole that he wouldn't sign off on his version of the story, which stated that the female had been driving the car. "Our whole relationship changed, and at that point, I was deemed—and became—a whistleblower," Hopson said. "The rapport I had with [my fellow officers] changed too."

Hopson had expected some hostility as a result of his action. Law enforcement officers are an insular group. They have one another's backs—for good and for bad—and Hopson understood that some would see his actions as a betrayal of a fellow officer. But Hopson never imagined the degree of unrelenting and systematic hostility and abuse he would face.

THE BLUE WALL

Police officers are famous for having one another's backs, both in the line of duty and outside of it. Some unwritten codes lie at the heart of their culture. Among them is the Blue Code of Silence, also called the Blue Wall or the Blue Shield, in reference to the standard blue color of the police officer uniform. According to this code, officers do not report other officers' mistakes or misdeeds. If questioned, an officer would claim ignorance rather than give testimony that would incriminate the fellow officer.

When Hopson refused to sign off on Cole's false report, he was putting justice ahead of the code. To the Lords of Discipline, that was an unforgivable offense. It made Hopson an outsider and untrustworthy in their eyes. Whether Hopson had been right or wrong didn't matter to them. All that mattered was that he had broken the code.

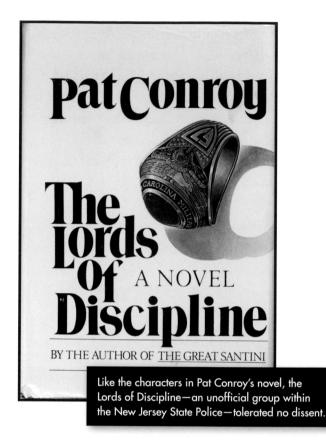

Like the characters in Pat Conroy's novel, the Lords of Discipline—an unofficial group within the New Jersey State Police—tolerated no dissent.

Within the state troopers was a loosely knit and highly secretive group of rogue officers who called themselves the Lords of Discipline. It was a name they had adopted from a novel by Pat Conroy that was also made into a movie. Conroy's story tells of a military college in which a small group of students known as the Lords of Discipline takes it upon themselves to discipline any student who steps out of line or doesn't fit in.

The members of the real-life group in the New Jersey police force harassed and punished officers who, in their view, were untrustworthy or unlikable. The group targeted Hopson for his unwillingness to support his training officer. Members wrote threatening notes and hit and shoved him in the halls. When he walked into a room, officers would get up and leave or fall silent. They vandalized his car and property. They shined spotlights on his house when he was sleeping.

Hopson referred to the abuse as the death of a thousand cuts, a type of slow torture practiced in ancient China. "I lived in a constant state of dread for months," he later wrote. And he worried about bigger consequences. What if, in the field, he needed the help of another officer? Could he count on an officer who happened to be a member of the Lords of Discipline to back him up? How far was the group willing to take the punishment?

> "I lived in a constant state of dread for months."
>
> —Justin Hopson, 2012

Blowing the Whistle

After several months, Hopson realized that the Lords of Discipline weren't going to leave him alone unless he quit the police force. But he didn't want to give up his dream job. So instead, in 2003 he agreed to help the state's attorney general's office and the New Jersey Task Force by providing evidence against the group as part of a formal and ongoing investigation. The investigation culminated in August 2003 with a court-martial of several men accused of running the Lords of Discipline. Hopson was the star witness, telling the court about the harassment and violence he had experienced in the months following the unlawful arrest. Defense lawyers tried to discredit him and paint him as an unreliable source, even trying to cast him as the liar in the case of the false DUI arrest. They badgered him on the witness stand, trying to trip him up and get him to contradict his story. But Hopson never wavered.

Hopson was hopeful that his testimony would change the culture of the New Jersey State Police. But while a few individuals were suspended from duty and the force itself was placed under federal oversight, the cultural change in the force that Hopson had been hoping for never came about. The abuse and isolation continued. Soon after the court-martial, Hopson gave in and walked away from his dream job.

In December 2003, Hopson filed a lawsuit against the state of New Jersey. The lawsuit stretched on for five long years. In the end, Hopson and the state agreed to a cash settlement of $400,000.

Hopson's case was one of the first in a series of legal challenges to the New Jersey State Police. From 2005 to 2012, troopers filed at least fourteen lawsuits against the state police, costing New Jersey taxpayers millions of dollars. Still, William Buckman, a lawyer who filed some of the lawsuits, said that little changed as a result of the lawsuits. That may be, in part, because not enough people have come forward.

"Integrity these days has become the exception rather than the rule. If we don't stand up to corruption, no one will."

—Justin Hopson, 2014

"I have interviewed many, many troopers who, after we've discussed their concerns, have decided not to become whistleblowers or not push an issue because their careers would be ruined and they would be retaliated against unmercifully," Buckman said.

Hopson has since moved to South Carolina to start anew. He has become a private investigator and an activist for whistle-blowers' rights. Hopson remains passionate about the importance of whistle-blowers. "Integrity these days has become the exception rather than the rule," he said. "If we don't stand up to corruption, no one will."

Chapter 6

In the Dark Shadows of College Football: Mike McQueary and the Penn State Abuse Scandal

Mike McQueary lived and breathed Pennsylvania (Penn) State University football. From 1994 to 1997, the Pennsylvania native was a quarterback for the Nittany Lions, the university's high-powered football team. He was the team captain in 1997 and led the Lions to the Citrus Bowl that season.

After college, McQueary pursued a professional football career. But after he failed to catch on with teams in the United States and Europe, it became clear that his dream of being a pro quarterback wasn't going to come true. It was time to turn to coaching. McQueary didn't have to look far for a job. In 2000 his former coach, Penn State legend Joe Paterno, offered McQueary a job as a graduate assistant on his coaching staff. It was an entry-level position. McQueary's role was to help Paterno and the other assistant coaches in any way he could. McQueary knew that Paterno had a history of promoting coaches from within his system.

While working as an assistant to Joe Paterno, head coach of the Penn State Nittany Lions football team, Mike McQueary *(above)* blew the whistle on assistant coach Jerry Sandusky for engaging in criminal sexual behavior. Like many whistle-blowing sagas, the case led to national scandal and destroyed personal and professional lives. It also sent a violent sexual predator to prison for life.

This meant that, with hard work, McQueary would have a good chance of climbing the coaching ranks. And that's exactly what he planned to do.

On the evening of February 9, 2001, McQueary was at home watching *Rudy* (1993), one of his favorite movies. The movie tells the tale of a Notre Dame football player who overcomes great odds to earn a spot on the team. Inspired by the film, McQueary returned to campus to pick up some videotapes of Penn State football recruits so he could scout their play and report his findings to Paterno and his staff. As soon as McQueary entered the coaches' locker room, it was clear that he wasn't alone.

In the shower room, McQueary heard what he later described as slapping sounds of a sexual nature. Through a mirror, he saw longtime Penn State assistant coach Jerry Sandusky, fifty-seven years old and slight of build, naked in the shower with a ten-year-old boy. In later testimony, McQueary was unclear about the specifics of what he did and did not see, but it appeared clear to him that something terrible was happening. Sandusky was raping the child.

McQueary, who later claimed to have suffered sexual abuse himself as a boy, was shocked by what he'd seen. Yet he was paralyzed by indecision. He made no move against Sandusky, either physically or verbally, nor did he rush to the boy's aid. He didn't remove the child from danger, and he did not call the police. When Sandusky became aware of McQueary's presence, the abuse stopped. But instead of confronting him, McQueary ducked into his office and then left the campus to think about what he'd witnessed.

In 2011 Penn State president Graham B. Spanier *(center)* resigned (the university's board of trustees claims he was dismissed) after a grand jury indicted coach Jerry Sandusky for sexually abusing minor boys. As of 2014, Spanier is still awaiting trial on charges related to the university cover-up of the scandal. The charges include eight counts of perjury, obstruction, and endangering the welfare of children, for which Spanier was indicted by a grand jury in 2012.

A Quiet Whistle

McQueary called his father to discuss what had happened, and his father urged him to talk to Paterno. So the next day, McQueary told Paterno what he'd seen. According to McQueary, Paterno replied, "I'm sorry you had to see that. It's terrible . . . I need to think and tell some people what you saw and I'll let you know what we'll do next . . . I know it's probably tough for you to come here and tell me this, but you've done the absolute right thing."

About ten days later, Paterno and McQueary reported the event to Penn State administrators, including university president Graham B. Spanier. Exactly what was said in the meeting remains a matter of debate. But according to McQueary, he made it clear to the administrators that the encounter between Sandusky and the boy was "extremely sexual." This was not the first report of sexual abuse that had been raised against Sandusky. He had been investigated for sexual abuse in the past, although none of the investigations had resulted in charges.

Yet despite McQueary's new accusations, his report went nowhere for nearly a decade. State laws mandate the report of sexual abuse, but Penn State administrators never reported the incident to the police or to the media, choosing instead to cover up the story. In addition, Spanier and others went to great lengths to ensure that the story would never see the light of day. Meanwhile, McQueary, Paterno, and others also quietly swept the incident under the rug, even though they too were bound by law to report the incident to authorities. Instead of reporting the abuse, the university banned Sandusky from bringing children onto the campus and left it at that. The curtain of silence was firmly in place to protect the image of Penn State football.

McQueary had blown the whistle. But he had done so as softly as possible.

Dark Secrets Come to Light

Over the next decade, McQueary rose up the ranks of the Penn State coaching staff. He took on a job as recruiting coordinator and receivers coach, learning the coaching ropes under Paterno. It seemed to many, including McQueary, that he was well on his way to a future job as a head coach.

But things began to change in 2010. Sandusky was once again being investigated for sexually assaulting young boys—a behavior that had persisted throughout the decade of silence. During this investigation, McQueary's brother, John, discussed Sandusky with a friend. John told the friend about what Mike McQueary had witnessed in 2001. The friend, recognizing the incident as a serious case of unreported child abuse, shared the information with the police, who then contacted Mike McQueary to interview him. After consulting with a lawyer, McQueary agreed to cooperate with the investigation against Sandusky. He became a key witness in the case, which quickly became a nationwide media story.

Accompanied by his defense attorney, Jerry Sandusky (*foreground*) speaks to the press in 2012. Sandusky met each of his victims through the Second Mile, a nonprofit charity he founded in the 1970s to help at-risk youth. As a result of the sex abuse scandal, the charity has folded.

Under Fire

Sandusky was widely vilified in the media for his alleged actions. But he wasn't the only one under fire. McQueary was also facing intense criticism as a result of his testimony. Some Penn State fans blamed him for tarnishing college football and the legacy of Paterno, a beloved, bigger-than-life personality. And it was hard for McQueary himself, who later said of his relationship with Paterno, "I love that man

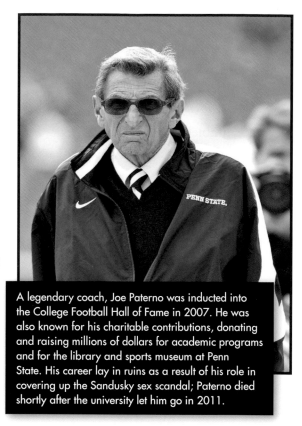

A legendary coach, Joe Paterno was inducted into the College Football Hall of Fame in 2007. He was also known for his charitable contributions, donating and raising millions of dollars for academic programs and for the library and sports museum at Penn State. His career lay in ruins as a result of his role in covering up the Sandusky sex scandal; Paterno died shortly after the university let him go in 2011.

more than you can ever possibly say. . . . He handled this thing in the best way he could. Was it foolproof or perfect? No. But I didn't handle this in a foolproof or perfect way either."

Other critics of McQueary were infuriated about what he hadn't done. They felt McQueary—whose powerful 6-foot-5 (2-meter), 215-pound (98-kilogram) frame towered over the much older and slighter Sandusky—should have had no problem stopping the rape and removing the boy from Sandusky's clutches. But he didn't do that. Nor did he call the police—an action he was ethically, morally, and legally obligated to take. He did report the incident to Paterno, but when the story was successfully hushed, he made no effort to revive it to make sure justice was served. To many, his inaction was unforgivable.

McQueary's personal life and once-promising career crumbled. He received death threats, which led the university to place him on indefinite paid administrative leave, having concluded he was a target on the sidelines of the football field. His marriage fell apart as well. Paterno too was facing the full brunt of the scrutiny for his own lack of initiative. The legendary coach was forced to resign in November 2011. He died of natural causes only months later.

"This is a tragedy. It is one of the great sorrows of my life. With the benefit of hindsight, I wish I had done more."

—Joe Paterno, 2011

New coach Bill O'Brien took over the Penn State football program in 2012. It is customary for a new coach to bring in his own coaching staff. O'Brien offered all of Paterno's assistant coaches—except McQueary—the opportunity to interview to keep their current positions under his regime. O'Brien told McQueary that his contract would not be renewed. McQueary's once-promising coaching career lay in ruins.

Unemployed, McQueary moved back into his parents' home. He searched for jobs without success. In October 2012, he sued Penn State for $4 million in lost wages, claiming that he had been dismissed unlawfully. In the lawsuit, McQueary alleges that he was fired because he blew the whistle on the university administration. A Pennsylvania whistle-blower law states that an institution cannot fire an employee for truthfully reporting to authorities cases of wrongdoing or waste.

Penn State officials countered with the argument that McQueary's firing had nothing to do with his role as a whistle-blower. They say it was a routine change in assistant coaches on a new staff. As of August 2014, the case remains unsettled.

With little chance of landing another job coaching football, McQueary turned to another passion, golf. During his attempts to pursue a career as a golf pro, McQueary tried to qualify for the 2014 US Open golf tournament. McQueary shot a 91, besting only two of some ten thousand hopefuls.

The Broader Impact

In the end, the state attorney general of Pennsylvania brought Sandusky to trial on forty-eight counts of child sexual abuse. In June 2012, a Bellefonte, Pennsylvania, jury found him guilty of forty-five of the counts—most of them felonies—with which he had been charged. That fall, in October 2012, Judge John Cleland delivered a sentence of thirty to sixty years in prison. As a sexually violent predator, Sandusky would be held in a maximum security prison. "This sentence will put you in prison for the rest of your life," Cleland told the sixty-eight-year-old Sandusky. Even after the conviction, a completely unremorseful Sandusky maintains his innocence.

The fallout didn't end with Sandusky's conviction. Former FBI director Louis Freeh conducted an independent investigation of the scandal and the cover-up. His report, released in July 2012, was a damning account of persistent abuse and willful cover-up by top Penn State administrators, reaching all the way to university president Spanier.

"They can take away my life, they can make me out as a monster, they can treat me as a monster, but they can't take away my heart. In my heart, I know I did not do these alleged disgusting acts."

—Jerry Sandusky, 2012

Sweeping changes followed. Spanier was forced to retire, while athletic director Tim Curley was fired outright. Later, Spanier, Curley, and other former school officials were charged with perjury for lying about what they knew while under oath and were charged for their roles in the cover-up. Their trial is pending. Spanier maintains his innocence and has sued Freeh for defamation.

Meanwhile, the National Collegiate Athletic Association (NCAA), which regulates top-level college athletics, came down hard on the Penn State football program. The NCAA imposed a $60 million fine, banned Penn State from postseason play for four years, and vacated all the school's victories from 1998 through 2011. In doing so, the NCAA wiped out Paterno's record as the winningest Division 1 football coach in history. The Big Ten Conference, to which Penn State belongs, imposed an additional $13 million fine. Penn State football had been brought to its knees and has not yet fully recovered.

Chapter 7

Traitor or Hero? The Edward Snowden Saga

In 2012 Edward Snowden—young, sharply intelligent, and passionate about personal freedom and liberty— was working in Hawaii as an information technology specialist for the US government's National Security Agency (NSA) as an employee of Dell, a private contractor that provides cybersecurity experts to US agencies. Snowden's position gave him access to highly classified NSA documents. And what Snowden saw in those documents concerned him deeply.

Coming into the job, Snowden had known that the NSA was involved in surveillance, collecting massive amounts of intelligence on both foreign and domestic threats—terrorism among them. Snowden, who had previously worked in a similar role with the CIA, understood that spying was a big part of what the NSA did. But Snowden had also believed that the organization set limits on the types of information it collected. Like most Americans, he assumed that the surveillance was targeted only at likely suspects.

Edward Snowden lives in exile in Moscow, facing charges of espionage in the United States for releasing confidential government documents.

Snowden soon realized that this was not the case. Over a period of months, he downloaded documents that proved that the NSA wasn't just spying on suspected terrorists. The agency was spying on just about everyone, from world leaders to ordinary citizens—and it was getting much of the information by tapping into resources such as Google, Yahoo, and private phone companies. Snowden felt that the breadth of the agency's spying was a threat to the liberty and to the right to privacy of Americans and all global citizens. He wanted the world to know what he had discovered, so he made a decision that would change his life forever. He was going to blow the whistle on the US government.

FRAMING THE DEBATE: PROTECTION OR INVASION?

Snowden revealed to the world that the NSA wasn't just spying on suspected terrorists. The agency was conducting mass surveillance—spying on almost everyone, both in the United States and abroad. The agency was collecting data on phone calls, e-mails, Internet use, and much more.

Snowden's revelations about the astonishing breadth of NSA surveillance sparked a heated debate about just what such programs mean to everyday, law-abiding citizens. NSA defenders claim that the agency needs the data to sniff out terrorist activity. The battle to root out terrorist activity is a little like finding a needle in a haystack, they argue. The NSA needs access to the entire haystack to find it. They argue that people who are doing nothing wrong have no reason to fear the surveillance. Only those actually engaging in illegal or threatening activities have any reason to fear.

Others disagree. They see such broad surveillance as unconstitutional and dangerous to a free society. While most people agree that some amount of surveillance is called for to protect US citizens from terrorism, critics argue that the agency greatly overstepped its bounds needlessly—and unlawfully—invading the privacy of millions.

The *Guardian* newspaper won the 2014 Pulitzer Prize for Public Service for the reporting Glenn Greenwald *(above)* and other *Guardian* journalists provided about the NSA surveillance program exposed by Edward Snowden. Greenwald, who is also a lawyer, has since written a book about his experience with Snowden. Documents discussed in the book, which is titled *No Place to Hide: Edward Snowden, the NSA, and the US Surveillance State*, are available online at no charge at http://www.glenngreenwald.net/#BookDocuments.

Code Name: Verax

Snowden knew that the NSA would take a very defensive, hostile stance toward any leak of the agency's deepest secrets. He even feared that by going public, he might be putting his life in danger. So before he whispered a word of what he knew, he took precautions, setting up anonymous online identities and doing all he could to cover his tracks. He operated under the code name Verax—Latin for "truth teller" and used strong encryption (password-protected) e-mails to make his connections with the journalists to whom he planned to tell what he knew.

In late 2012 and early 2013, when Snowden felt that his identity was safely hidden, he reached out to newspaper reporter Glenn Greenwald of the *Guardian,* a British newspaper, and to Berlin-based American documentary filmmaker Laura Poitras.

Both had reported on government surveillance in the past, so Snowden felt they would have a handle on the explosive information he possessed. Soon after that, in May 2013, he got in touch with journalist Barton Gellman, then working for the *Washington Post*. Gellman is a Pulitzer Prize–winning journalist known for his reporting on the September 11 terrorist attacks on the United States. In broad terms, Snowden told his contacts what he knew

Filmmaker and journalist Laura Poitras focuses much of her work on the United States in the post-9/11 era. Part of a trilogy, her 2006 film *My Country, My Country* looked at life in Iraq during the American occupation. The film was nominated for an Academy Award in 2007. The second film in the trilogy, *The Oath*, tells the stories of Abu Jandal, Osama bin Laden's former bodyguard, and Salim Hamdan, a prisoner at the US military prison at Guantánamo Bay, Cuba, who is facing war crimes charges. The third film will look at NSA mass surveillance.

and the scope of the documentation he could provide, asking them to help tell the story.

Snowden and Gellman planned a face-to-face meeting for mid-May 2013, where Snowden would hand over forty-one PowerPoint slides detailing an NSA surveillance operation called PRISM. This classified program secretly tapped into data banks of Internet giants such as Google and Facebook to gather information about people all over the world. With this information, the NSA could track a person's Internet usage, interpersonal friend networks, communications, and more.

The meeting with Gellman would mark a point of no return for Snowden. Shortly before the meeting, he wrote a message to Gellman clarifying that he accepted the personal consequences of his whistle-blowing. "I understand that I will be made to suffer for my actions, and that the return of this information to the public marks my end. . . . You can't protect [me], but if you help me make the truth known, I will consider it a fair trade. . . . There's no saving me."

Dropping the Bomb

Snowden applied for and received a medical leave of absence from his job, claiming he needed time off to receive treatment for epilepsy. Then, on May 20, 2013, Snowden left Hawaii for Hong Kong. He didn't even tell his girlfriend where he was going.

At the meeting with Gellman, Snowden handed over some of his documentation. The *Washington Post* published only a fraction of what Snowden had provided, holding back some of the most sensitive material. It was a bitter disappointment to Snowden, who had hoped

Barton Gellman is an award-winning journalist who has written about the global AIDS pandemic, the September 11 terrorist attacks, the global war on terror, and secret US intelligence operations. He led the *Washington Post* coverage of the NSA surveillance program exposed through confidential documents leaked to him by Edward Snowden.

the story would make a much bigger media splash. Frustrated with Gellman, Snowden turned to other sources, including the *Guardian*. Snowden provided media outlets all over the world with document after document, all of which implicated both the United States and its allies, especially Great Britain, in a massive surveillance program that targeted many countries, from China to Brazil to Mexico. Perhaps even more damaging was the revelation that the NSA's programs had specifically targeted dozens of world leaders, including German chancellor and US ally Angela Merkel. The response to the leaked information was dramatic, and the story exploded as headline news around the world.

A BALANCING ACT

Snowden's actions, along with several other high-profile whistle-blowing cases involving the US military and its intelligence agencies, have brought the question of whistle-blower protections to the forefront. Whistle-blower rights have proven to be a tricky issue for legislators and other political leaders.

President Barack Obama, in particular, faced a difficult situation in the wake of Snowden's revelations. During his 2008 presidential campaign, Obama had championed whistle-blower rights, boldly calling for federal employees to step forward and expose wrongdoing. Yet once in office as chief executive, Obama was compelled to protect US interests and to give intelligence agencies the tools they feel they need to combat terrorism. Many people in the intelligence community feel that Snowden jeopardized the ability of the NSA and other agencies to do effective work in the fight against terrorism. For that reason, President Obama has backed away from some of the promises he made in relation to whistle-blower rights, earning heavy criticism from many who had supported him on the issue.

On June 9, 2013, from his Hong Kong hotel room, Snowden revealed his identity to the world in a video interview with Greenwald and Poitras. He explained his actions. "I'm willing to sacrifice [all that I have] because I can't in good conscience allow the U.S. government to destroy privacy, Internet freedom, and basic liberties for people around the world with this massive surveillance machine they're secretly building," he said. "I don't see myself as a hero, because what I'm doing is self-interested. I don't want to live in a world where there's no privacy and therefore no room for intellectual exploration and creativity."

With that, the chase was on. The US government was determined to capture and arrest Snowden for multiple counts of espionage and theft of government property. Altogether, the counts could potentially put him behind bars for the rest of his life. So Snowden did all he could to stay a step ahead of his pursuers.

Cat and Mouse

Snowden had chosen Hong Kong for a reason. He knew that because the United States and China have a long history of distrust and lack of cooperation Chinese officials would not be eager to hand him over. But he couldn't stay in Hong Kong forever. As US agents closed in on his location, he made new plans, this time with the help of WikiLeaks and its founder, Julian Assange. Famous for uncovering and going public with sensitive, often classified documents, Assange was eager to help.

Initially, Snowden planned to travel to Ecuador to seek political asylum, or protection from prosecution. The nation had already granted asylum to Assange and seemed a perfect destination for Snowden. On June 23, unknown to US agents, Snowden boarded an airplane to Moscow, Russia. The capital city was not initially Snowden's intended final destination, but the US government revoked his passport, essentially stranding him in Moscow.

Once Snowden was in Russia, the United States pressured the Russians to hand him over. President Obama vowed to use all legal means necessary to extradite Snowden and to force him to face the charges against him. But the Russian government, already in a shaky relationship with the United States, refused to do so. The two nations faced a diplomatic standoff.

Snowden continued to search for options. He applied for asylum to more than twenty nations, including France, Germany, and Cuba. The game of cat and mouse stretched into July, when the nation of Bolivia vowed to give Snowden asylum, if he could only reach its borders. But Snowden remained trapped in the Moscow airport. Finally, on August 1, Russia granted him temporary asylum for one year. More than one month after his arrival, Snowden was finally allowed to leave the airport.

In the months that followed, Snowden continued to work with media sources, releasing more and more damaging information on PRISM. He released additional materials about other NSA programs as well, including more details about how the NSA had spied on world leaders—including those of US allies. Meanwhile, Snowden remained mostly behind the scenes. In a December 17, 2013, interview with Gellman, Snowden indicated that his mission was complete. "I am not trying to bring down the NSA," he explained. "I am working to improve the NSA. . . . They are the only ones who don't realize it."

WIKILEAKS

The website WikiLeaks is devoted to uncovering and publishing secret and classified information. Australian journalist and publisher Julian Assange *(below)* founded the site in 2006 as a way to battle corruption in world governments as well as in private industry. The site gained international attention in 2010 when it published more than seventy-six thousand classified military documents, mainly concerning the US military's war in Afghanistan.

Since then, WikiLeaks and Assange have published hundreds of thousands of additional documents from all over the globe. While Edward Snowden did not use WikiLeaks to reveal the data he had collected, Assange and other WikiLeaks activists did help him flee Hong Kong and also tried to help him secure political asylum. Assange is currently living and working from the Ecuadorian Embassy in London, having been granted the protection of political asylum from Ecuador in 2012.

WikiLeaks founder Julian Assange speaks to the media inside the Ecuadorian embassy in London on June 14, 2013, nearly a year after seeking refuge there.

"Given that the threat [of terrorism] is growing, I believe that [removing surveillance programs] is an unacceptable risk to our country. Taking these programs off the table, from my perspective, is absolutely not the thing to do."

—*General Keith Alexander, NSA chief, 2013*

Snowden was hailed by many in the United States as a hero. Yet the war of words wasn't entirely one-sided. While Snowden continued to condemn the actions of the NSA, some in the US intelligence community grew increasingly critical of Snowden. Some called him a spy. Others said he had been working for Russia all along. One of his most vocal critics was US Representative Mike Rogers of Michigan, chairman of the US House Intelligence Committee. Rogers suggested that Snowden had been paid by Russia for the confidential information, acting out of profit motives rather than civic concern. "[Snowden] has contacted a foreign country and said, 'I will sell you classified information for something of value,'" Rogers said in a December 2013 interview. "That's what we call a traitor in this country."

The Snowden Effect

For Snowden personally, his decision to blow the whistle on the NSA has forever changed his life. On a positive note, he has been hailed as an international hero, garnering international awards, such as the German Whistleblower Prize, as well as the Sam Adams Award, given by a group of retired CIA officials in recognition of an intelligence professional who has made a stand for ethics and integrity. Snowden was named the *Guardian*'s Person of the Year in 2013 and was runner-up for the same honor in *Time* magazine. Yet despite the honors and recognition, Snowden has also become an international fugitive. He may never be able to return home, and if he does, he's likely to stand trial and potentially serve a long sentence for crimes against his own country.

Snowden remains in Russia, which has since agreed to extend his asylum. He remains on the forefront of the battle for privacy protection. In 2014 he joined the board of directors for the Freedom of the Press Foundation and was also elected rector (a leading academic official) of the University of Glasgow in Scotland.

The fallout extends far beyond one man, however. The so-called Snowden Effect has had wide-ranging impact on the NSA and on surveillance agencies around the world. For example, formal investigations into the NSA's programs have been launched both within the US government and abroad. Programs that before Snowden's revelations went largely without oversight have suddenly been subject to far greater scrutiny than ever before. Lawmakers immediately began looking at reform. In 2013, for example, Minnesota senator Al Franken introduced a bill called the Surveillance Transparency Act. The law would require the NSA and other agencies to disclose far more information about the data they collect. And in early 2014, President Obama called for an expert review of the programs utilized by the NSA and other intelligence agencies, with the vow of serious reform.

The Snowden Effect has also hit the technology industry. Major Internet portals such as Google, Facebook, and Twitter have faced heavy criticism, as well as financial backlash from lost users, for their role in the PRISM program. It remains unclear exactly how the NSA accessed personal data through these sites. Either the portals gave the agency full access or they didn't do enough to protect the data. Either way, argue some consumer rights activists, they let down users.

"There is a huge difference between legal programs, legitimate spying . . . and these programs of dragnet mass surveillance that put entire populations under an all-seeing eye. . . . These programs were never about terrorism: they're about economic spying, social control, and diplomatic manipulation. They're about power."

—Edward Snowden, 2013

The Snowden Effect has led to a change in the ways many people around the world view and use technology, especially the Internet. Since 2013 many companies and private citizens have turned to high-level encryption software and the use of identity-masking tools such as proxy servers to disguise a user's true location when accessing the Internet. And increasingly, foreign governments are making plans to splinter the World Wide Web into numerous national Internets as a way of protecting against the kind of external surveillance Snowden revealed. Many critics, however, fear these moves will hamper the original goal of the Web as a free and borderless forum for easily connecting users around the globe to information.

In the end, Snowden achieved what he set out to do. He made all Americans—and people around the world—aware of massive unauthorized, behind-the-scenes surveillance. And he forced the beginnings of reforms that could result in increased privacy protections for everyone around the globe. According to Snowden, the loss of his own freedom was a small price to pay.

Epilogue

Democratic societies have a wide range of institutions and mechanisms for exposing corruption, illegal actions, and dark secrets to protect citizens from harm. These tools include the three branches of government, laws and other forms of legislation, legally mandated reporting across a range of social institutions, the police, the media, and the democratic process of electing officials to office. But those institutions and mechanisms aren't always up to the task, and like any human organization, they can be vulnerable to the same forces of corruption they are meant to expose and protect against. For this reason, many scholars point to whistle-blowers as another necessary and vital arm of democratic society. In a paper written for the International Whistleblower Research Conference, hosted by Middlesex University in London in June 2011, political philosophy expert Abraham Mansbach wrote that "by disclosing wrongdoing that results in public harm, all the forms of whistleblowing protect the community, promote the public good, and extend the rule of law."

> "By disclosing wrongdoing that results in public harm, all the forms of whistleblowing protect the community, promote the public good, and extend the rule of law."
>
> —political philosopher Abraham Mansbach, 2011

Blowing the whistle can have far-reaching consequences for the good of any society, democratic or not. It can change the way people view the world around them. It can right wrongs. It can expose corruption and send wrongdoers to prison. But it can also destroy careers and lives. Is it worth it?

Edward Snowden has described his decision to step forward as easy. But that doesn't mean he is without regrets. "The only thing I fear is the harmful effects on my family, who I won't be able to help anymore," Snowden says. "That's what keeps me up at night."

When *60 Minutes* interviewed Jeffrey Wigand in 1996, his life was in complete turmoil. His career had all but ended. His marriage was falling apart. His future was very much in doubt. "There are times I wish I hadn't done it," he admitted during the interview. "But there are times that I feel compelled to do it. If you asked me if I would do it again or . . . do I think it's worth it? Yeah. I think it's worth it. I think in the end people will see the truth."

Justin Hopson agrees. "If I had to do it all again, I would," he said. "I lost a career that I found so rewarding and worked so hard to attain . . . but when it comes to integrity and honesty, there's really no gray area. We all know right from wrong. It's easy for someone to say they would stand up [to expose injustice], but very few people have the fortitude to do it. It takes a hero. It takes someone with strong character to stand up and buck the system."

WHO'S WHO?

The stories in this book are just a few of the many instances of whistle-blowing courage in US history. Below are five additional cases. You can learn more about them and about other whistle-blowers at the National Whistleblowers Center (NWC) website (http://www.whistleblowers.org). The NWC is a nonprofit, nonpartisan organization dedicated to protecting employees' lawful disclosure of waste, fraud, and abuse.

Pauline DeWenter

In early December 2013, Pauline DeWenter, a scheduling clerk with the Veterans Affairs (VA) hospital in Phoenix, Arizona, called US Navy veteran Thomas Breen. She wanted to let him know that an appointment had finally opened up for him at the hospital. Breen's daughter-in-law angrily informed DeWenter that he had just died. Breen had been waiting for months to receive care. That moment on the phone was a turning point for DeWenter, who has since gone public to blow the whistle on the cover-up of patient neglect at the Phoenix hospital. She charges that records of dead veterans were altered to disguise that as many as forty veterans died while waiting for care and that new requests for treatment were systematically ignored. In June 2014, the FBI opened a criminal probe to further investigate the Veterans Affairs Department and the charges related to the VA scandal.

Daniel Ellsberg

Daniel Ellsberg worked as a strategic analyst for the RAND Corporation (a California-based policy research and analysis institution) during the Vietnam War (1957–1975). Ellsberg's job gave him access to classified documents (later known as the Pentagon Papers) that suggested, among other things, that the war was not winnable. The documents also exposed the US government's unauthorized, secret expansion of its military involvement in the war. In March 1971, Ellsberg shared the papers with *New York Times* reporter Neil Sheehan, and the papers went public. Ellsberg faced trial on charges of espionage, conspiracy, and theft. His trial was dismissed, however, due to illegal gathering of evidence and gross governmental misconduct. Ellsberg's exposure of the Pentagon Papers contributed to the disintegration of public support for the war, eventually leading to the end of US military involvement in Vietnam.

Cate Jenkins

In 2006 Cate Jenkins—a chemist for the Environmental Protection Agency (EPA)—blew the whistle on the agency. She explained to the media that the agency knew about and covered up information about the toxicity of the dust released from the collapse of the World Trade Center towers on September 11, 2001. The EPA chief assured the public that the contaminants from 9/11 dust were minimal. However, studies from the US Geological Survey supported Jenkins's claims. Subsequent research revealed that as many as two-thirds of firefighters and other rescue teams at the site had suffered permanent lung damage. The damage could have been prevented had the workers been provided with proper protective gear. Jenkins was fired by the EPA in late 2010 on the grounds that she had threatened her supervisor. Jenkins sued under the federal Whistleblower Protection Act, and in 2012, she was reinstated with back pay.

Chelsea (formerly Bradley) Manning

In 2010 Chelsea (born Bradley) Manning, intelligence analyst for the US Army, leaked hundreds of thousands of classified military documents to the WikiLeaks website. The site publishes leaks and other secret information. Among other things, the material revealed that the US government had vastly underreported the number of civilian casualties in the US-led wars of the early 2000s in Iraq and Afghanistan. The material also included thousands of US State Department cables, which are viewed as the most damaging information from a diplomatic point of view. The cables revealed that ally nations held views about the wars that were sometimes quite different from those they shared in public. Manning was arrested and later charged under the Espionage Act with aiding the enemy. Manning pleaded guilty in 2013 to ten of twenty-two charges and is serving a thirty-five-year prison sentence.

Frank Serpico

In April 1970, New York City police officer Frank Serpico reported to the *New York Times* that Brooklyn police officers were accepting bribes and payoffs from criminals. Mayor John

Lindsay formed a commission to investigate Serpico's charges. The commission carried out the most extensive investigation of police misconduct in New York City history and exposed corruption and cover-up that led to widespread departmental reform. After blowing the whistle, Serpico was shot in the face during a drug raid. Fellow officers on the scene did not respond to his calls for help (a neighbor did). Serpico retired from the police department in 1972 after receiving its highest honor, the Medal of Honor. Actor Al Pacino won a Golden Globe award for Best Actor for his performance as Frank Serpico in the popular 1973 film *Serpico*. The film tells the story of Serpico's experience blowing the whistle on police corruption.

TIMELINE

1777 Delegates to the American Continental Congress draft one of the world's first laws to protect whistle-blowers.

1970s Consumer-protection activist Ralph Nader coins the term *whistle-blower* as a more positive word for "snitch," to refer to someone who exposes confidential information.

1972 In May and again in June, burglars break into and bug the headquarters of the Democratic National Committee at the Watergate office complex in Washington, DC. On June 19, Bob Woodward and Carl Bernstein of the *Washington Post* report that one of the men who had been arrested, James McCord Jr., was in charge of security for President Richard Nixon's reelection and fund-raising organization. With the help of a whistle-blower known only as Deep Throat, the journalists eventually uncover a story of presidential corruption and cover-up.

1974 Facing impeachment as a result of the Watergate scandal, President Nixon announces to the nation on live television on August 8 that he will resign from office, effective at noon the next day.

1989 The Whistleblower Protection Act is enacted to protect US federal employees from retaliation for reporting unlawful or unethical conduct.

1993 Brown &Williamson (B&W) fires research and development executive Jeffrey Wigand for bringing to light that the tobacco company was repressing information that documented the addictive properties of tobacco as well as its known health risks.

1996 On February 4, after a long delay, CBS airs Mike Wallace's full interview with Wigand on *60 Minutes*. In the tell-all exposé, Wigand explains that tobacco executives have ignored health concerns and lied about the dangers they know to be associated with smoking.

1998 The attorneys general of forty-six states and four major US tobacco companies agree to the Tobacco Master Settlement Agreement. As part of the deal, B&W drops its lawsuit against Wigand. The tobacco companies agree to restrict tobacco marketing to youth as well as to annual payments in the billions of dollars to the states in the lawsuit.

1999 Former police officer Kathryn Bolkovac travels to Bosnia to begin work as a monitor with the International Police Task Force, a United Nations (UN) peacekeeping force. Her job is to work with women and children who had been raped during the ethnic war (1992–1995) in the former Yugoslavia, as well as with postwar victims. She is fired after revealing what she knows about sex trafficking among UN peacekeepers.

2001 Sherron Watkins, a vice president of corporate development at the offices of Enron Corporation, reveals gross financial fraud at the company. Mike McQueary, an assistant for the Penn State football coaching staff, observes assistant coach Jerry Sandusky in a sex act with a young boy in the coaches' locker room showers. The next day, McQueary reports what he has seen to Joe Paterno. The university chooses to do nothing.

2002 New Jersey state trooper Justin Hopson observes his training officer make an unlawful arrest. Hopson refuses to sign off on the officer's official report of the arrest and faces months of harassment for this decision from an unofficial group of troopers known as the Lords of Discipline.

2003 The UN enacts a zero-tolerance policy for peacekeepers who commit crimes of a sexual nature. In New Jersey, trooper Justin Hopson participates in an investigation that culminates in a court-martial of several men accused of running the Lords of Discipline. Hopson leaves the police force and files a lawsuit against the state of New Jersey for the harassment he has endured.

2005 Mark Felt, former associate director of the FBI, reveals in *Vanity Fair* magazine that he is the Deep Throat of Watergate fame.

2008 The state of New Jersey agrees to pay Justin Hopson a cash settlement of $400,000.

2012 McQueary loses his job at Penn State and sues the university for $4 million in lost wages, claiming that he had been dismissed unlawfully. A Bellefonte, Pennsylvania, jury finds Sandusky guilty of forty-five of the forty-eight counts of child sex abuse—most of them felonies—with which he had been charged. As a sexually violent predator, he is sentenced to thirty to sixty years in prison.

2013 Edward Snowden provides journalists with documents showing a massive surveillance program of global citizens on the part of the US National Security Agency. Facing charges of espionage, he flees to Moscow. Later in the year, he is named the *Guardian* newspaper's Person of the Year and is runner-up for the same honor in *Time* magazine.

2014 Snowden joins the board of directors for the Freedom of the Press Foundation and is elected rector (a leading academic official) of the University of Glasgow in Scotland.

SOURCE NOTES

7   Stephen M. Kohn, "The Whistle-Blowers of 1777," *New York Times*, June 12, 2011, http://www.nytimes.com/2011/06/13/opinion/13kohn.html?_r=0.

7   Ibid.

13 Sherron Watkins, "Truth . . . Why Is It Difficult?" *The Insufferable Truth Blog*, October 28, 2008, http://www.sherronwatkins.com/sherronwatkins /Insufferable_Truth_Blog/Entries/2008/10/28_Truth...._why_is_it_difficult .html.

18 Todd S. Purdum, "Ronald L. Ziegler, Press Secretary to President Nixon, Is Dead at 63," *New York Times*, February 12, 2003, http://www.nytimes .com/2003/02/12/us/ronald-l-ziegler-press-secretary-to-president-nixon-is -dead-at-63.html.

20 Bob Woodward, *The Secret Man: The Story of Watergate's Deep Throat* (New York: Simon & Schuster, 2005), 5.

21 David Von Drehle, "FBI's No. 2 Was 'Deep Throat': Mark Felt Ends 30-Year Mystery of the *Post*'s Watergate Source," *Washington Post*, June 1, 2005, http://www.washingtonpost.com/politics/fbis-no-2-was-deep-throat-mark -felt-ends-30-year-mystery-of-the-posts-watergate-source/2012/06/04 /gJQAwseRIV_story.html.

21 "Deep Throat Revealed," *Washington Post*, May 31, 2005, http://www .washingtonpost.com/wp-srv/politics/special/watergate/part4.html.

22 Carroll Kilpatrick, "Nixon Tells Editors, 'I'm Not a Crook,'" *Washington Post*, November 18, 1973, http://www.washingtonpost.com/wp-srv/national /longterm/watergate/articles/111873-1.htm.

24 Associated Press, "Ex-FBI Official: I'm Deep Throat," *NBC News*, June 1, 2005, http://www.nbcnews.com/id/8047258/ns/us_news/t/ex-fbi-official-im-deep -throat/#.U2f-qhB7Skw.

25 Lloyd Grove, "Bernstein, Woodward Swat Down 'Leak' Questioning Deep Throat's Motive," *Daily Beast*, April 9, 2012, http://www.thedailybeast.com /articles/2012/04/09/bernstein-woodward-swat-down-leak-questioning-deep -throat-s-motive.html.

30 Robert W. Butler, "Jeffrey Wigand, Rising from the Ashes." *Kansas City Star*, November 21, 1999, http://articles.baltimoresun.com/1999-11-21 /entertainment/9911230630_1_jeffrey-wigand-tobacco-michael-mann.

30 Danish Raza, "Tobbacco Activist Jeffry Wigand Says Whistleblowing Has Become His Calling," *Firstpost*, September 12, 2013, http://www.firstpost .com/business/tobbacco-activist-jeffry-wigand-says-whistleblowing-has -become-his-calling-1103343.html.

31 "Jeffrey Wigand on *60 Minutes*, February 4, 1996 [transcript]," *Jeffreywigand .com*, accessed January 24, 2014, http://www.jeffreywigand.com/60minutes .php.

33 "Battling Big Tobacco," *60 Minutes*, January 13, 2005, http://www.cbsnews .com/news/battling-big-tobacco.

37–38 Daniel McGrory, "Woman Sacked for Revealing UN Links with Sex Trade," *Prison Planet*, August 7, 2002, http://www.prisonplanet.com/woman_sacked _for_revealing_un_links_with_sex_trade.html.

38 Lia Petridis Maiello, "When Peacemakers Become Perpetrators: Kathryn Bolkovac Introduces *The Whistleblower* at the UN," *Huffington Post*, February 19, 2013, http://www.huffingtonpost.com/lia-petridis/the-whistleblower -author-interview_b_2663231.html.

38 Kathryn Bolkovac, *The Whistleblower: Sex Trafficking, Military Contractors, and One Woman's Fight for Justice* (New York: Palgrave MacMillan, 2011), 129.

39 Ibid.

44 Justin Hopson, telephone interview with the author, February 7, 2014.

45 Ibid.

47 Justin Hopson, *Breaking the Blue Wall: One Man's War against Police Corruption* (Bloomington, IN: WestBow Press, 2012), 26.

48 Hopson interview.

49 Christopher Baxter, "Troopers' Lawsuits against State Police Cite Transfers, Lost Promotions," *Newark Star-Ledger*, September 23, 2012, http://www .nj.com/politics/index.ssf/2012/09/troopers_lawsuits_against_stat.html.

49 Ibid.

53   Don Van Natta Jr., "The Whistleblower's Last Stand," *ESPN The Magazine*, March 4, 2014, http://espn.go.com/espn/feature/story/_/id/10542793/the-whistleblower-last-stand.

54   Ibid.

56   Ibid.

57   "Joe Paterno to Retire; President Out?," *ESPN.com*, November 9, 2011, http://espn.go.com/college-football/story/_/id/7211281/penn-state-nittany-lions-joe-paterno-retire-end-season.

58   Candace Smith, Beth Loyd, and Colleen Curry, "Jerry Sandusky Gets 30 to 60 Years for Sex Abuse after Tearful Victim Statements," *ABC News*, October 9, 2012, http://abcnews.go.com/US/jerry-sandusky-sentenced-30-60-years-prison/story?id=17427234.

59   "Full Statement from Jerry Sandusky Maintaining Innocence on Sex-Abuse Charges," *NBC News*, October 8, 2012, http://usnews.nbcnews.com/_news/2012/10/08/14301078-full-statement-from-jerry-sandusky-maintaining-innocence-on-sex-abuse-charges?lite.

65   Barton Gellman, "Code Name 'Verax': Snowden, in Exchanges with *Post* Reporter, Made Clear He Knew Risks," *Washington Post*, June 9, 2013, http://www.washingtonpost.com/world/national-security/code-name-verax-snowden-in-exchanges-with-post-reporter-made-clear-he-knew-risks/2013/06/09/c9a25b54-d14c-11e2-9f1a-1a7cdee20287_story.html.

67   "Edward Snowden: The Whistleblower behind the NSA Surveillance Revelations," *Guardian* (London), June 9, 2013, http://www.theguardian.com/world/2013/jun/09/edward-snowden-nsa-whistleblower-surveillance.

68   Barton Gellman, "Edward Snowden, after Months of NSA Revelations, Says His Mission's Accomplished," *Washington Post*, December 23, 2013, http://www.washingtonpost.com/world/national-security/edward-snowden-after-months-of-nsa-revelations-says-his-missions-accomplished/2013/12/23/49fc36de-6c1c-11e3-a523-fe73f0ff6b8d_story.html.

70   Margaret Ledwith, "NSA: Metadata Collection Is Key Weapon against Terrorism," *State Column*, December 11, 2013, http://www.statecolumn.com/2013/12/nsa-metadata-collection-is-key-weapon-against-terrorism/.

70   Benjamin Bell, "Rep. Mike Rogers: I'd Pay for Edward Snowden's Ticket Back to US to Face Charges," *ABC News*, December 22, 2013, http://abcnews .go.com/blogs/politics/2013/12/rep-mike-rogers-id-pay-for-edward-snowdens -ticket-back-to-u-s-to-face-charges/.

72   Bradley Brooks, "NSA's Indiscriminate Spying 'Collapsing,' Snowden Says in Open Letter," *Washington Post*, December 17, 2013, http://www .washingtonpost.com/world/nsas-indiscriminate-spying-collapsing-snowden -says-in-open-letter/2013/12/17/ecfcdad6-674f-11e3-8b5b-a77187b716a3_story .html.

74   Abraham Mansbach, "Whistleblowing as Fearless Speech: The Radical Democratic Effects of Late Modern Parrhesia," in *Whistleblowing and Democratic Values* edited by David Lewis and Wim Vandekerckhove; published by the International Whistleblowing Research Network, Social Science Research Network, 2011, http://papers.ssrn.com/sol3/papers.cfm?abstract _id=1998293.

75   Glenn Greenwald, Ewen MacAskill, and Laura Poitras, "Edward Snowden: The Whistleblower behind the NSA Surveillance Revelations," *Guardian* (London), June 9, 2013, http://www.theguardian.com/world/2013/jun/09/edward -snowden-nsa-whistleblower-surveillance.

75   "Jeffrey Wigand on *60 Minutes*, February 4, 1996," *Jeffreywigand.com*, February 4, 1997, http://www.jeffreywigand.com/60minutes.php.

75   Hopson interview.

91   Street Law, Inc., "Nixon's Views on Presidential Power: Excerpts from a 1977 Interview with David Frost," streetlaw.org, n.d., http://www.streetlaw.org/en/ Page/722/Nixons_Views_on_Presidential_Power_Excerpts_from_a_1977 _Interview_with_David_Frost.

SELECTED BIBLIOGRAPHY

Bolkovac, Kathryn. *The Whistleblower: Sex Trafficking, Military Contractors, and One Woman's Fight for Justice*. New York: Palgrave MacMillan, 2011.

Gellman, Barton. "Code Name 'Verax': Snowden, in Exchanges with *Post* Reporter, Made Clear He Knew Risks." *Washington Post*, June 9, 2013. http://www.washingtonpost.com/world/national-security/code-name -verax-snowden-in-exchanges-with-post-reporter-made-clear-he-knew -risks/2013/06/09/c9a25b54-d14c-11e2-9f1a-1a7cdee20287_story.html.

———. "Edward Snowden, after Months of NSA Revelations, Says His Mission's Accomplished." *Washington Post*, December 23, 2013. http://www .washingtonpost.com/world/national-security/edward-snowden-after-months -of-nsa-revelations-says-his-missions-accomplished/2013/12/23/49fc36de-6c1c -11e3-a523-fe73f0ff6b8d_story.html.

Gjelten, Tom. "Officials: Edward Snowden's Leaks Were Masked by Job Duties." *National Public Radio*, September 18, 2013. http://www.npr.org/ 2013/09/18/223523622/officials-edward-snowdens-leaks-were-masked-by -job-duties.

Greenwald, Glenn, Ewen MacAskill, and Laura Poitras. "Edward Snowden: The Whistleblower behind the NSA Surveillance Revelations." *Guardian* (London), June 9, 2013. http://www.theguardian.com/world/2013/jun/09/ edward-snowden-nsa-whistleblower-surveillance.

Hopson, Justin. *Breaking the Blue Wall: One Man's War against Police Corruption*. Bloomington, IN: WestBow Press, 2012.

Lyman, Rick. "A Tobacco Whistle-Blower's Life Is Transformed." *New York Times*, October 15, 1999. http://www.nytimes.com/1999/10/15/us/ a-tobacco-whistle-blower-s-life-is-transformed.html?ref=jeffreywigand.

Van Natta, Don, Jr. "The Whistleblower's Last Stand." *ESPN.com*, March 4, 2014. http://espn.go.com/espn/feature/story/_/id/10542793/the -whistleblower-last-stand.

"The Watergate Story, Part 4: Deep Throat Revealed." *Washington Post*, May 31, 2005. http://www.washingtonpost.com/wp-srv/politics/special/watergate/part4.html.

Wetzel, Dan. "Mike McQueary, Broken Down and Estranged, Files $4 Million Whistleblower Lawsuit." *Yahoo! Sports*, October 2, 2012. http://sports.yahoo.com/news/ncaaf--mike-mcqueary-estranged--files-4-million-whistleblower-lawsuit.html.

Woodward, Bob. *The Secret Man: The Story of Watergate's Deep Throat.* New York: Simon & Schuster, 2005.

FOR FURTHER INFORMATION

Books

Bacon, John U. *Fourth and Long: The Fight for the Soul of College Football.* New York: Simon & Schuster, 2014. A best-selling author, Bacon looks at the world of major college football, giving a gripping account of the scandals and inner workings of four Big Ten schools—Penn State, Ohio State, Michigan, and Northwestern.

Behnke, Alison Marie. *Up for Sale: Human Trafficking and Modern Slavery.* Minneapolis: Twenty-First Century Books, 2015. This title examines human trafficking around the world, from forced agricultural labor and domestic servitude to sex and adoption trafficking and the human organ trade. *Up for Sale* looks at legal reforms, international conventions, the work of advocacy groups, and the human drama of victims and perpetrators alike.

Bernstein, Carl, and Bob Woodward. *All the President's Men.* New York: Simon & Schuster, 1974. These two *Washington Post* journalists published this account of their investigative reporting of the Watergate scandal just two months before President Richard Nixon resigned from office. It became the basis for a classic American political thriller movie of the same name, released in 1976.

Bolkovac, Kathryn. *The Whistleblower: Sex Trafficking, Military Contractors, and One Woman's Fight for Justice.* New York: Palgrave Macmillan, 2011. Bolkovac recounts her harrowing experiences in Bosnia, detailing how she learned about rampant human sex trafficking among international peacekeepers and the obstacles she faced in exposing it.

Fremon, David K. *The Watergate Scandal in American History.* Berkeley Heights, NJ: Enslow, 2014. Fremon offers a detailed look at the most famous political scandal in US history and how it changed the way Americans view government.

Hopson, Justin. *Breaking the Blue Wall: One Man's War against Police Corruption.* Bloomington, IN: WestBow Press, 2012. Whistle-blower Justin Hopson offers a detailed account of his clash with the Lords of Discipline.

Jones, Phill. *Freedom of Information.* New York: Chelsea House, 2012. This title discusses government transparency, civilians' rights to privacy, and the delicate balance between protecting essential state secrets while preserving civic rights.

Kemper, Bitsy. *The Right to Privacy: Interpreting the Constitution.* New York: Rosen, 2014. Kemper discusses the ways in which the US Constitution protect citizens' rights to privacy.

Kluger, Richard. *Ashes to Ashes: America's Hundred-Year Cigarette War, the Public Health, and the Unabashed Triumph of Philip Morris.* New York: Vintage, 1997. Journalist and social historian Richard Kluger takes a comprehensive look at the history of tobacco, from early Native American usage through the Big Tobacco lawsuits of the 1990s. Kluger won the Pulitzer Prize for this voluminous yet highly readable book.

Mollenkamp, Carrick, Jeffrey Rothfeder, Adam Levy, and Joseph Menn. *The People vs. Big Tobacco: How the States Took on the Cigarette Giants.* Princeton, NJ: Bloomberg Press, 1998. In a blow-by-blow account, this book describes how a coalition of top American trial lawyers and state attorneys general took on the tobacco industry, eventually resulting in a multibillion-dollar settlement against Big Tobacco.

Websites

Edward Snowden's Life as We Know It
http://abcnews.go.com/Blotter/timeline-edward-snowdens-life/
story?id=19394487
ABC News traces the life of Edward Snowden from birth through his
intelligence career, including his decision to blow the whistle on the NSA and
to exile in Russia.

A *Guardian* Guide to US Government Whistleblowers
http://www.theguardian.com/world/interactive/2013/jun/24/guardian
-guide-us-government-whistleblowers#Snowden
The *Guardian* takes a brief look at influential whistle-blowers in recent history,
including Edward Snowden, Mark Felt, and many others.

Inside the Tobacco Deal
http://www.pbs.org/wgbh/pages/frontline/shows/settlement/timelines/
fullindex.html
In 1998 PBS's *Frontline* ran an exposé of the lawsuit that brought down Big
Tobacco. The site provides the transcript of the documentary along with a
useful timeline of events.

National Whistleblowers Center
http://www.whistleblowers.org/
This nonprofit organization fights to protect workers' legal rights to lawfully
disclose fraud, waste, and abuse. Read thrilling whistle-blower biographies,
check out whistle-blower protections by state, and read the latest news on the
subject at this site.

10 Whistleblowers and the Horrors They Exposed
http://people.howstuffworks.com/10-whistleblowers-and-the-horrors-they
-exposed.htm#page=0
This site takes a look at the whistle-blowing phenomenon and focuses
on the stories of ten famous whistle-blowers, what they exposed, and the
consequences they faced.

US Department of Labor Whistleblower Protection Programs
http://www.whistleblowers.gov/
The Occupational Safety & Health Administration's Whistleblower Protection Program is built to inform workers of their rights and to enforce laws designed to protect those who come forward. At this site, would-be whistle-blowers can learn more about their rights, how to protect themselves legally, and find out where to go for help.

Films

All the President's Men. DVD. Directed by Alan J. Pakula. Burbank, CA: Warner Home Video, 1976. Based on the uncovering of the Watergate scandal, this film tracks the story of investigative journalists Bob Woodward (played by Robert Redford) and Carl Bernstein (Dustin Hoffman) and their work with a mysterious source, Deep Throat (Hal Holbrook), to track the scandal to its source in the White House.

David Frost Interviews Richard Nixon. DVD. Directed by Jørn Winther. Los Angeles: Liberation Entertainment, 2008. In 1977 British journalist and television host David Frost conducted a series of twelve interviews with Richard Nixon three years after the president's resignation. The immensely popular and riveting interviews were televised in the United States and other countries around the world. In the interviews, Nixon never admits guilt, famously stating that "when the president does it that means that it is not illegal." The interviews later became the basis of a play and a movie, both titled *Frost/Nixon.*

The Insider. DVD. Directed by Michael Mann. Burbank, CA: Touchstone Home Video, 2000. This Academy Award–nominated film starring Russell Crowe as Jeffrey Wigand tells the story of Wigand and his efforts to expose the industry secrets of Big Tobacco.

The Whistleblower. DVD. Directed by Larysa Kondracki. Los Angeles: 20th Century Fox, 2012. This film takes an unflinching look at the horrors uncovered by Kathryn Bolkovac in Bosnia, as well as her struggles to bring them to light. Rachel Weisz plays Bolkovac.

INDEX

PHOTO ACKNOWLEDGMENTS

The images in this book are used with the permission of: © badahos/
Shutterstock.com, (backgrounds); © Barton Gellman/Getty Images, p. 5;
© Kean Collection/Getty Images, p. 6; © Laura Westlund/Independent
Picture Service, p. 10; © PixelPro/Alamy, p. 13; Chuck Kennedy/KRT/
Newscom, p. 14; Gregory_Heisler/epa/Newscom, p. 15; © Bettmann/
CORBIS, pp. 17, 19; © Everett Collection/Alamy, p. 23; FRED PROUSER/
REUTERS/Newscom, p. 27; Tyler Anderson/National Post/ZUMApress/
Newscom, p. 35; © Alexandra Wyman/Getty Images, p. 40; © Justin Hopson,
p. 43; © Todd Strand/Independent Picture Service, p. 46; © Chris Szagola/
ZUMA Press/CORBIS, p. 51; © Christopher Weddle/Centre Daily Times/
MCT/Getty Images, p. 53; © Pat Little/Retuers/CORBIS, p. 55; Mike
McAtee/ZUMAPRESS/Newscom, p. 56; © Barton Gellman/Getty Images,
p. 61; AP Photo/Silvia Izquierdo, p. 63; © AP Photo/Charles Sykes/Invision,
p. 64; AP Photo/J. Scott Applewhite, p. 65; Anthony Devlin/AFP/Getty
Images/Newscom, p. 69.

Front cover and jacket: © Dragonimages/Dreamstime.com, (people);
© badahos/Shutterstock.com.

ABOUT THE AUTHOR

Author and editor Matt Doeden has written hundreds of children's and young adult books on topics ranging from history to sports to current events. His titles *Sandy Koufax, Tom Brady: Unlikely Champion,* and *The World Series: Baseball's Biggest Stage* were Junior Library Guild selections. His title *Darkness Everywhere: The Assassination of Mohandas Gandhi* was among the Best Children's Books of the Year by the Children's Book Committee at Bank Street College. Doeden lives in Minnesota with his wife and two children.